CW00961032

Ugborough
DEVON

Culgaith
CUMBRIA

Hampton-in-Arden
WARWICKSHIRE

Rokeby
DURHAM

Great Dunmow
ESSEX

Aldershot
HAMPSHIRE

Woburn Sands
BEDFORDSHIRE

Aldeburgh
SUFFOLK

Sedbergh
NORTH YORKSHIRE

lest we forget

war memorials

Peter Ashley

ENGLISH HERITAGE

AN ENGLISH HERITAGE POCKET BOOK

P 4 **Cenotaph** LONDON
See p 31

Edward Thomas's poem *The Private* appears on page 73, and my grateful thanks go to
Mrs Myfanwy Thomas, the poet's youngest daughter.

Published by English Heritage, Kemble Drive, Swindon SN2 2GZ
www.english-heritage.org.uk
English Heritage is the Government's statutory adviser on all aspects of the historic environment.

© Peter Ashley
Images © Peter Ashley.

First published 2004

ISBN 1 85074 911 6

Product code 50961

British Library Cataloguing in Publication data
A CIP catalogue record for this book is available from the British Library.

All rights reserved
No part of this publication may be reproduced or transmitted in any form or by any means,
electronic or mechanical, including photocopying, recording, or any information storage or
retrieval system, without permission in writing from the publisher.

Edited by Val Horsler
Page layout by Peter Ashley and Chuck Goodwin
Cover by Peter Ashley

Printed by Bath CPI

contents

introduction   8

monumental   10

architectural   32

typographical   42

sculptural   44

additional   60

As with others in this series of books, *Lest We Forget* can only be an introduction to its subject. Whilst I have made special expeditions to photograph particular memorials, most were collected on my travels around certain Engish counties. I am very aware that it has been impossible to give a proportionate geographic spread, and there is nothing here from the rest of the British Isles, which of course played an essential part in the conflicts. Missing too are the magnificent and moving memorials abroad, particularly in Northern France.

The book is divided into five sections: *Monumental* looks at the bold statements that include those influenced by mausolea, obelisks and columns; *Architectural* looks at buildings; *Typographical* is a brief look at lettering styles; *Sculptural* takes in soldiers and other statues; and we finish with *Additional*, a random selection including the more curious.

introduction

'…the men leaving the gardens tidy / The thousands of marriages lasting a little longer: / Never such innocence again.' MCMXIV by Philip Larkin

Only a handful remain of the thousands who queued in 1914 to enlist in the British Army in, as Larkin says in this same poem, *'…long uneven lines / Standing as patiently / As if they were stretched outside / The Oval or Villa Park…'* – a sentiment of lost innocence still holding true for those who fought in another conflict, a second World War 25 years later.

It is difficult to write of something so devastating, so horrific, as the multiple deaths of so many. I was born 34 months after VE Day, so it was not until the early 1950s that I became conscious of what had happened, of a war that still shadowed our lives. I wondered why I went to school on a 1930s bus, why a factory wall in Leicester stood in gaunt isolation with glassless windows framing a white-tiled basement, open to the sky and framed in rosebay willowherb, the 'fireweed' of bomb sites. Later, I wondered who the soldiers were who stared out at me from picture frames angled on top of great aunts' pianos and bureaux. Soldiers in itchy khaki photographed against studio backdrops that already looked like dark-curtained corners of a sepia afterlife, silently drawing me to the realisation that there had been another war, an earlier hell. And the realisation that these soldiers were something to do with the names I'd seen on the local war memorial.

There is a Crimean War memorial in Woolwich, and Boer War memorials can be found dedicated to the ordinary servicemen who served from 1899–1902, but by far the most ubiquitous are those erected in the aftermath of the First World War. The government of the time refused to acknowledge the concept of the repatriation of the dead, so these monuments became the focal points for grief. In the absence of graves and headstones the cross, church lych gate, garden of remembrance or village hall marked the passing of whole swathes of the population.

There are of course many reminders that specifically commemorate the dead of the Second World War, but usually the names of individuals were added to existing memorials. These memorials were raised by public subscription, by generous donations. But as the intervening years lengthen, a mute indifference to these monuments now threatens their existence. The charity Friends of War Memorials receives information on around 300 cases of neglect a year as memorials decay and suffer vandalism and even destruction. Some end up in skips and there has even been a mindless trade in them on the internet.

English Heritage are helping by providing grants for their restoration, and as wartime anniversaries bring renewed interest in the countless acts of bravery they celebrate, so awareness of these sorrowful monuments grows once again in villages and towns. We will all be aware of our local memorial; we should all make sure we get involved in preserving it for future generations. But very importantly we should remember what caused them to be there. Look beyond the names and imagine the boys, the girls, the sons, the parents. The loud sergeants, the shy corporals. The grocers, the clerks. The signalmen, the ticket collectors. And never forget the flash of steel, the crump of the shell, the suddenness of the bullet that engraved their names in front of you.

monumental

Victoria Park LEICESTER

This was the first war memorial I knew, the destination for Remembrance Sunday parades drumming their way up to the wide open spaces of Victoria Park from Leicester's city centre. It is a classic entry in Edwin Lutyens' portfolio of uncompromising monuments, a towering Portland stone arch of 1923 with his signature flattened dome, forbiddingly ring-fenced with railings stretched between piers decorated with funerary swags and vases. And motionless flags in painted stone.

Brookwood SURREY

The London Necropolis Company founded the Brookwood Cemetery in 1854 in direct response to the crippling overcrowding of London's churchyards caused by an unprecedented population explosion. The 2,400 acres of Surrey heathland provided such an expanse of burial grounds they even had their own funeral railway running out of Waterloo to two separate stations amongst the pines.

Within these acres is the military cemetery, remarkable for the classical American Mausoleum, by McKim, Mead & White, that stands so pale against the trees, looking out over the regimented rows of tombstones. The landscaping and works were carried out by a New York designer with the remarkable name Egerton Swartout.

Brookwood SURREY

The Brookwood Memorial of 1958 commemorates those with no known resting place, 3,500 casualties from the Second World War, with a simple circle with radiating fins that take the bronze name plaques.

Tucked away in the shade of the trees is an Italian section, where lie prisoners of war. These cemeteries are spread over 37 acres, and are the largest military burial grounds in the United Kingdom.

< **Constitution Hill** LONDON

The Commonwealth Memorial commemorates the men and women from the Commonwealth countries who served in two World Wars. Four Portland stone pillars with shallow urns form a guard-of-honour gateway on Constitution Hill, with the roadway between them paved with red granite setts from India. In the ceiling of the domed pavilion are inscribed the names of those Commonwealth men awarded the Victoria Cross and George Cross. This is a very recent memorial, designed by Liam O'Connor Architects and opened by Her Majesty the Queen in November 2002.

> **Bedford**

War Memorials will often be found in the environs of barracks. This is the Bedfordshire & Hertfordshire Regimental Memorial that sits opposite The Keep, originally the Kempston Barracks in Bedford. The left-hand pillar is inscribed with the names of those lost in the First World War; the right-hand pillar is for the Second. Behind the classical domed pavilion with its iron door is a garden of remembrance. Bedford typifies so many town memorials, in our peripheral vision as we hurtle about our business. Perhaps this monument gets a more appreciative glance when the traffic grinds to a halt on the Kempston Road.

THEIR · NAME · LIVETH · FOR · EVERMORE

15

THE MEN OF BURWASH

EVERMORE

Burwash EAST SUSSEX

Burwash is quintessential southern England. Tile-hung houses, pollarded limes lining brick paths, a church with a broach spire roofed with shingles. And down a lane that descends into the valley of the River Dudwell, a 17th-century ironmaster's house, Batemans, home to Rudyard Kipling.

The writer who penned the line 'Lest We Forget' had an only son, John, who was rejected for army service at the outbreak of the Great War because of his appalling eyesight, but his father used his influence to bypass the military red tape and secure him a commission. Second Lieutenant John Kipling was killed at the Battle of Loos on the 27th September 1915. Heavy with remorse, his father spent the rest of his life roaming the battlefields and cemeteries of northern France looking for his son's grave. Kipling died in 1936 without accomplishing his mission, but what is not often included in this tragic story is the fact that the son was as keen as the father to go to war for his country.

A grave was found in 1992 at the St Mary's Dressing Station Cemetery near Loos that supposedly contains John Kipling's body, but there is apparently still conjecture about it. One thing is certain: John's name is inscribed on this characterful little stone tower by St Bartholomew's church.

∧ **Rousdon** DEVON

Here was the family seat of the Peeks, of Peek Frean biscuits fame. The war memorial sits hidden in the shade of trees at the side of the A3052 Lyme Regis to Seaton road, and doubles up as a local milestone.

⊐ **Lower Swell** GLOUCESTERSHIRE

Edwin Lutyens worked here on alterations to a Victorian country house, Abbotswood, his most extensive foray into the Cotswolds. Twenty years later his work appeared in Lower Swell again, this time for the war memorial with its classical flaming urn – a reminder that this prolific architect, whose name will forever be indelibly linked to the most imposing post-Great War memorials, was also capable of designing something so comfortably in scale with a small Gloucestershire village.

> **Rushden** NORTHAMPTONSHIRE
Rushden is typical of the Nene
Valley towns between
Northampton and Thrapston that
once owed their living to the boot
and shoe industry. Walk the streets
of these red brick towns and
villages and you will find terraces of
Victorian houses grouping
themselves around tall factories like
hens around chicken feeders, the
stuff of early H E Bates' novels.
Rushden was his boyhood home.

Amongst the stock brick is the
local ironstone, the dark
gingerbread that yields black
currants of ore that once fed the
roaring furnaces of Corby
steelworks. St Mary's church in
Rushden uses it to great effect,
mixing it with a paler local
limestone. Less dramatic, but a
perfect foil to the church tower, is
the octagonal war memorial
opposite. Remembered at the core
of their community, the clickers and
welters, the outworkers from back
garden 'barns' and their families,
friends, fellow townspeople from a
river valley in the heart of England.

Stretton-on-Dunsmore WARWICKSHIRE

This obelisk will be familiar to anyone driving along the A45 between Coventry and Daventry or down to the south west from Leicester to Cirencester on the Fosse Way. The old Roman road cuts across the grain of England, and where it meets the dual carriageway at Knightlow Hill this memorial stands on a roundabout.

It commemorates the assembling here of the 9th Regiment of the British Army between December 1914 and March 1915. On the 12th March George V inspected the troops before they departed for Gallipoli. Many of the soldiers had been billeted locally, and 7,000 people gathered here to watch the unveiling of their monument on Tuesday 24th May 1921.

Meriden WARWICKSHIRE

In 1972 Stephen Frears directed a film that plotted an excursion in 1911 by a group of cyclists into the Yorkshire countryside. Written by Alan Bennett, *A Day Out* ended with the depleted ranks of the cycling club paying their respects to their fallen comrades as they stood bareheaded around a war memorial (in reality the one in Ackroyden Square in Halifax) on Armistice Day in 1919.

On seeing this grim monolith in Meriden, the Cyclists' Memorial, I thought how this film was a more fitting reminder of the cyclists who died in the Great War, and indeed those of the Second World War who joined them here on a tacked-on plate. I think it's because *A Day Out* is about the living, men so full of life, hope, expectancy; pedalling and joshing their way unwittingly towards the immense shadow of the unknown.

It's a great pity that something more imaginative couldn't have been erected here, not only because this is the self-styled centre of England, but also because it stands in the nexus of the great names of the cycling and motorcycling industry.

Elveden SUFFOLK

A landmark for travellers crawling up the A11 to Norwich, this 100-foot fluted column towers over the surrounding Breckland pines. Three parishes meet here: Eriswell, Icklingham and Elveden itself, and here we are on the 23,000 acre agricultural estate that was so remarkably developed out of the sandy heaths by the Earl of Iveagh, of Guinness fame. In the 1950s this vast estate was the largest arable farm in England.

The column, designed by Clyde Young and erected in 1921, has stairs ascending to the almost obligatory urn, but these are now blocked up. It would have provided a rare panoramic viewpoint of these strange tree-silhouetted East Anglian acres and of the recent burning down of a nearby holiday village.

Clevedon NORTH SOMERSET

A simple and unusual red marble column on the seafront of this Somerset resort on the Severn Estuary. The dove is in a curious position as if toppling from the column with the weight of the wreath.

Swanbourne BUCKINGHAMSHIRE

Polebrook NORTHAMPTONSHIRE

Burnham-on-Crouch ESSEX

Chelmondiston SUFFOLK

Somerset House LONDON

Another Lutyens design, this time for the Civil Service Rifles, with static flags and carefully incised lettering in creamy limestone, stands in front of one of the arches on the riverside frontage of Somerset House, once the registry of the country's births, marriages and deaths. The urn takes the eye up to one of the bearded river gods that adorn the keystones, whilst the column tells us of the 1,240 members that lost their lives in the Great War. In appropriate Civil Service fashion their names were written out on a scroll that was placed inside the column.

I first saw it from a vantage point on Waterloo Bridge one bright January day, and on going down to the Strand I found that Somerset House was undergoing a major restoration programme. On making enquiries I was taken out to the river front and shown the memorial which had literally just that morning been unveiled after its own restoration. I had to move a hosepipe out of the way to take my photograph. I mention all this because it was indeed a rare opportunity to see a war memorial exactly as it would have originally appeared.

MCM
XIX

IN MEMORY
OF THE
1240 MEMBERS
WHO FELL
WHILE SERVING
WITH
THE REGIMENT
IN
THE GREAT WAR

THEIR NAMES
ARE RECORDED
ON A SCROLL
PLACED WITHIN
THIS COLUMN

ALSO IN MEMORY
OF MEMBERS OF
THE CIVIL SERVICE
CADET BATTALION

FESTUBERT 1915. LOOS. SOMME 1916. 1918. FLERS. COURCELETTE.

Snape SUFFOLK

Two classical columns stand guarding an altar-like memorial with its stone wreath.

No echo here of the church of St John the Baptist, in whose churchyard it lies, with its colourful patchwork of flint and red roof pantiles. Both church and memorial are now a little way out of the village that gathers around the quay on the River Alde where an impressive range of old maltings stands in red brick and white weatherboarding. One of the largest is now the concert hall so inextricably entwined with the Aldeburgh Festival and its founder Benjamin Britten, who wrote the *War Requiem* that so hauntingly counter-pointed Wilfred Owen's immortal poetry: *And no guns thumped, or down the flues made moan.*

Stoke Albany NORTHAMPTONSHIRE

If not churchyards and town squares, then village greens. A space for the young, tipping out of school, yelling and scuffling across the grass; a space for the old who watch them at their games, remembering. And for those who grew not old, their names inscribed in stone by the lettercutter as carefully as they were first inked onto birth certificates, the school register, Sunday School prizes, pay packets and then, with the obligatory number, the dehumanising barcode of the military, onto enrolment papers held out for the confirming signature.

Cenotaph LONDON

The physical core of a nation's remembrance in Whitehall. November Sunday mornings, leaves scurrying in the silence as London's traffic hums in the distance. Black overcoats, red poppies. Chill breezes teasing flags and gently playing with white hair.

'Cenotaph' is Greek for an empty tomb, a sepulchral monument for bodies elsewhere. Edwin Lutyens learnt of the name from his great friend and collaborator Gertrude Jekyll, and subsequently pointed it out to Lloyd George when the latter briefed the architect on a 'catafalque' to be the focus for the Victory parade on 19th July 1919.

A permanent memorial was commissioned from him on 30th July in the same year, and construction commenced once Lutyens had won a battle with those who wanted a giant granite cross. The geometry is spectacularly complex, filling, as Lutyens commented to Vita Sackville West, 33 pages of his notebook. There isn't a perfectly upright horizontal or vertical line in it. Lutyens brought sculptural qualities to plain blocks of stone; if the vertical lines were continued upwards they would meet at an imaginary point 1,000 feet above the memorial. And likewise all the horizontals are arcs of a circle whose centre is 900 feet underground.

architectural

<< **Penrith** CUMBRIA

This Penrith war memorial is a pink sandstone version of the
churchyard lychgate. 'Lych' is an Anglo-Saxon word meaning
'corpse' and lych gates were designed to be a covered porch
beneath which the coffin rested on a bier for a few minutes, a
sort of symbolic momentary pause between this life and the next.
Penrith's gate is between the railway station and a public park,
and, although built well into the 20th century, the whole design is
Victorian Gothic, right down to the 12th-century medieval
alphabet spelling out one of the standard war memorial texts
around the pointed arch.

< **Loughborough** LEICESTERSHIRE

Loughborough is the home of a world famous bell foundry.
The John Taylor Founders have cast bells here since 1784,
including the largest bell in Britain, the prodigious 'Great Paul'
which weighs in at 37,483 lbs and swings sonorously in St Paul's
Cathedral. How fitting, then, that Loughborough's War Memorial is
this red brick campanile. This was the first 'grand carillon' in Britain,
erected in 1923 in Queens Park to commemorate the 480 men
of the town who lost their lives in the 1914–18 war.

A carillon differs from normal bellringing practice (ie: pulling bell-
ropes) in that the bells are rung by playing a keyboard like a
church organ. The 47 bells are hung in the copper belvedere at a
height of 151 feet above the rooftops of the town, each bell
appropriately inscribed. The inaugural recital included a Memorial
Chime by Sir Edward Elgar, composed specially for the event.

Oundle NORTHAMPTONSHIRE

Oundle School is such an integral part of this beautiful stone-built town that it is sometimes difficult to disentangle its buildings from the surrounding fabric of houses and shops. Which is all to the good, as this factor above all else has helped to preserve the town's essential character. But just up from the centre on Milton Road we can be in no doubt that we are in the presence of wealth and its intendant privileges.

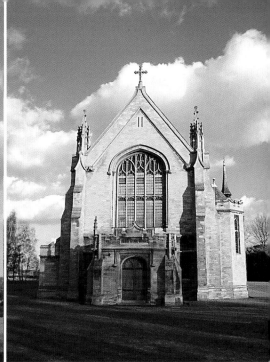

This is the school chapel, able to stand in glorious isolation from other buildings, a worthy testament to the ethos of the school, but more importantly to those from its high-collared and coat-tailed ranks who went from cricket fields to battlefields and lost their lives. This entire building is a war memorial, built here in 1922–3 to the Perpendicular designs of A C Blomfield. In 1956 stunning stained glass by John Piper was made by Patrick Reyntiens and installed in the apse.

Crich DERBYSHIRE

There have been view towers on Crich Stand since the 18th century, when the first was erected by the Hurts of Alderwasley in 1788. Visitors to the National Tramway Museum below will know of the 1923 successor, an inland lighthouse perched 1,000 feet above sea level on the precipitous edge of an old stone quarry. This is the memorial to the 11,409 Sherwood Foresters who served and fell in the Great War, and to those of subsequent conflicts. The site is significant because the regiment was made up of men from both Derbyshire and Nottinghamshire, and Crich Stand is close to the border of both counties. The lighthouse was officially opened on an August afternoon in 1923 as a vast crowd sang 'O God Our Help in Ages Past'.

Of course, a site as prominent as this has always seen beacon fires lit over the centuries, and as the Derbyshire skies darken at the end of the day the flashing beacon should always be looked out for as one traverses the hills between Alfreton and Wirksworth.

SHERWOOD FORESTERS

NOTTS & DERBY

1914 - 1918

1939 - 1945

THE MEMORY OF 11409 MEN OF ALL RANKS OF THE
RWOOD FORESTERS (NOTTINGHAMSHIRE AND DERBYSHIRE

THIS TABLET IS ERECTED IN
GRATEFUL REMEMBRANCE OF
THE THIRTY MEN OF YARDLEY
HASTINGS WHO GAVE THEIR ✝
LIVES IN THE GREAT WAR
1914 - 1919

ARTHUR ASHLEY
TIMOTHY ASHLEY
FREDERICK CECIL ASHLEY
RICHARD WILLIAM ALLSOPP
CHARLES CARTER
HERBERT CARTER
THOMAS EDWARD CARTER
GEORGE JAMES DOWNING
HAROLD EVANS
THOMAS WILLIAM FRAZEL
HARRY GIBSON
GEORGE KING
JOSEPH JAMES KING
ALBERT LACK
GEORGE WILLIAM PARTRIDGE
EDWIN ROSE
FREDERICK ROUSE
GEORGE ROBINSON
JAMES WILLIAM ROBINSON
ROWLAND CECIL TEARLE
FREDERICK UNDERWOOD
GEORGE UNDERWOOD
SYDNEY JOHN UNDERWOOD
WALTER UNDERWOOD
WALTER WILLIAM UNDERWOOD
GEORGE WEST
FREDERICK WHITNEY
WALLACE WHITNEY
ALBERT WOODING
CHARLES WILLIAM WOODING

SO THEY PASSED OVER,
ALL THE TRUMPETS S
FOR THEM ON THE O

IN FREEDOMS CAUSE
1939 - 1945

HUBERT PARTRIDGE
ROBIN MINNEY
ALFRED PICTON

< ∧ **Yardley Hastings** NORTHAMPTONSHIRE

Up and down the country the word 'Memorial' was tacked on to many on-going projects, not the least being the village hall. Here in a village a mile and a half from both the Bedfordshire and Buckinghamshire borders the war memorial is an integral part of the building. My great-grandfather was the carrier here, rumbling with his cart every day between Northampton and Bedford, and the names on the plaque kick off with three Ashleys. When I photographed the hall I remembered a family story that a favourite trick of the contemporary Yardley youth was to drag the chain up out of the village well late at night and drape it round the door latches of workers' cottages, denying them their early morning exits. I wonder if any of these names were amongst the perpetrators.

⌐ **Bodmin** CORNWALL

A clock tower at a road junction in Bodmin commemorates the lives of members of staff at the local Cornwall Mental Hospital who died in two world wars. One imagines the use this landmark is put to in giving directions out of Bodmin: 'Just take the right-hand fork at the clock tower, then you're straight on for Wadebridge'.

Waterloo LONDON

Waterloo Station is alone amongst London termini in not having an immediately apparent main entrance. Having another railway line running directly in front of it doesn't help. Most passengers will arrive here either by Underground or taxi, so this façade is only seen by those straying out in the direction of Waterloo Bridge. But it should be seen, and appreciated, because it doubles up as the London & South Western Railway's War Memorial to its staff. By the steps descending to street level are the sombre bronze rolls of honour name plaques and outside obelisk lamp standards flank a monumental arch that is inset with plaques denoting theatres of war: Dardenelles, Mesopotamia, Egypt – very distant destinations from the home stations of the LSW&R and their employees: Evercreech Junction, Broad Clyst, Witley for Chiddingfold.

typographical

Mercantile Marine Memorial TRINITY SQUARE, LONDON

VICTORY
1914 – 1918

Apethorpe NORTHAMPTONSHIRE

1914-1918

Hampton-in-Arden WARWICKSHIRE

MAKE TH

Achurch NORTHAMPTONSHIRE

IN VAIN
THAT THEIR NAME
BE NOT FORGOTTEN
ND WHAT THEY STROVE FOR
PERISH NOT

H. A. R. NORTON
W. H. OSBORNE
J. G. PAYNE
C. W. PIMM
E. E. PINCHES
G.
J. W. POWELL
T. A. PRINCE

Lichfield STAFFORDSHIRE

sculptural

< **Bedford**

A Boer War soldier in full overseas kit dominates the yard in front of the Swan Hotel, a hostelry built in 1794 for the Duke of Bedford. Down here Bedford still manages to maintain the atmosphere of a riverside town, and one can imagine the youths at the start of George V's reign laughing their way down to the Ouse for a boating party. What did they think of this soldier standing proudly in the sun? Did they ever dream how soon they too could be in uniform?

<< **Stokesay** SHROPSHIRE

When you next come to visit Stokesay Castle, take a look in the churchyard next door at this pink sandstone moustachioed soldier. It is thought that he was modelled on illustrator Bruce Bairnsfather's 'Old Bill', the seen-it-all-before soldier who lightened the rigours of trench life with his philosophic humour.

The giant fish held behind his back has always seemed vaguely comical, but there are a number of cogent reasons for its appearance on memorials. Christians have of course appropriated stylised fish as part of their corporate identity, and they are found in Greek mythology as a transport for dead heroes. Many naval badges and memorials rely on it, but here in Stokesay it may be a reference to the King's Shropshire Light Infantry, raised in 1755, who served as a maritime regiment in the Seven Years War.

Conisbrough SOUTH YORKSHIRE

This soldier in his puttees (strips of heavyweight cloth wound round the legs for support) advances watchfully. A timeshift to our own century could easily transform him into one of today's icons, the musician with his Fender Stratocaster, an image about as removed from the horror of the Great War as this determined private is from the 12th-century military strategies that played out behind him in Conisbrough Castle.

Port Sunlight MERSEYSIDE

A memorial for the soap makers. Port Sunlight is the creation of William Hesketh Lever who built this self-contained model community after his Sunlight soap became brand leader in 1887. Here we find the plans of over 30 architects stretched out over neatly-lawned acres, styles that include arts and crafts vernacular and a Victorian interpretation of a roseate past. Standing at a crossroads at the centre of the 'village' heroic bronze soldiers guard their comrades and defend the women and children of this idealistic home front. The memorial is by Sir W Goscombe John.

Hyde Park Corner LONDON

The Royal Artillery Memorial is one of the most dramatic, and, on its unveiling in 1925, one of the most criticised of Great War monuments. The sheer brutality of war is self-evident here. A Howitzer gun is not rendered any less potent by being carved out of a giant chunk of Portland stone, its barrel ratcheted up to create exactly the right angle of fire to drop a shell onto the Somme. The men leaning against the plinth are as real. Battle-hardened, they stand with the heavy accoutrements of their deadly trade, leaning up against the stones above their dead comrade who lies covered by a greatcoat that overhangs the inscription: 'Here was a Royal Fellowship of Death.'

The main structure, which took four and a half years to build, was the responsibility of architect Lionel Pearson, but the sculptor was Charles Sergeant Jagger, himself no stranger to the battlefield. He abandoned a career at the Royal College of Art to join the Artists' Rifles in 1914. The horrors of Gallipoli marked him forever, and after being wounded in 1915 he returned to the Western Front to suffer gas attacks in the trenches of Flanders and severe wounds at the Battle of Neuve Eglise. He was awarded the Military Cross for bravery in 1918.

TO THE MEMORY OF
THE BURBAGE MEN,
WHO GAVE THEIR LIVES FOR THEIR COUNTRY
1914 — 1919.

2ND LIEUT. A.W. DUDLEY.
2ND LIEUT. H.S. PILGRIM.
2ND LIEUT. W.G. ROBINSON.

PTE. J.D. ADKIN.	PTE. H. JAMES.
" J.L. ALDRIDGE.	" E.H.G. KELSEY.
" J.R. ARNOLD.	" R.G. KELSEY.
" J.H. ASBURY.	L.CPL. G.S. KIRBY.
" J. ALSOP.	PTE. W.H. LETTS.
" B. BATES.	" S.H. MUSSON.
" F. BURTON.	" P. MALKIN M M
" H. BASS.	" J. MOORE.
" C. BARNES.	" W. NEAL.
" F. BARNES.	" A.J. PAUL.
" C. BRADBURY.	" J. PAUL.
" W. BRADSHAW.	" G. ROWLEY.
" H. CHARLES.	" B. ROBINSON.
" D. CHARLES.	" D. ROBERTSON.
" T. CAMPTON.	" B. ROWE.
CPL. J. COOK.	" G.N. SCOTT.
PTE. A. COOK.	" P. STARKEY.
L.CPL. T. COX.	" A.E. SMITH.
PTE. C.J. CHAMBERLAIN.	" L. SHILTON.
" S.C. FOXON.	" A. SMITH.
" F. FORRYAN.	CPL. J. TOWERS.
" J. GRIMES.	L.CPL. W. WORMLEIGHTON.
" A.H. GHENT.	PTE. H. WORMLEIGHTON.
" J. HILL.	" W. WEBSTER.
L.CPL. T.H. HAMLET.	" F. WYLES.
PTE. W. HINTON.	

"GREATER LOVE HATH NO MAN THAN THIS, THAT
A MAN LAY DOWN HIS LIFE FOR HIS FRIENDS."

Burbage LEICESTERSHIRE

The houses may change with the weather, TV aerials, double glazing, rendering, loft conversions; but still there is the fixed point, the focus, the soldier and all that he stands to attention for. Burbage is no different from thousands of villages across the land; the work may be different (here it was hosiery), but the lists of names with their impersonal initials are Burbage people husbands, boyfriends, fathers, sons – and a girl in the WRAF. In this village on the edge of Hinckley many will still know the names, perhaps even the faces from rigidly-posed sepia photographs. The genes carry on, the family trees are drawn out, the websites (with digital bugles playing the Last Post) flash the lists across the world. The names now become people again, the people who left the village to become Privates, Drivers, Sappers, Fusiliers. And here in Burbage a Squadron Leader.

Alnwick NORTHUMBERLAND

Soldiers stand in eternal vigil at the foot of a
lantern-topped column, on the crest of a hill
where the Great North Road stretches away
south to the rest of England and north to
Scotland. The bowed stance of the cast figures
is immediately redolent of the human tableaux
that dutifully guard the remains of those
granted a traditional lying-in-state.

Euston Station LONDON

Another vigil by four bronze figures outside
Euston Station, this time commemorating
railway workers. The stone obelisk on a granite
base is one of the survivors of the original
station environs that includes the twin lodges on
the Euston Road with their incised destinations
on the quoins. The memorial is by Reginald
Wynn Owen and was erected here in Euston
Square in 1921.

National Memorial Arboretum STAFFORDSHIRE

A detail from a memorial to Phoenix staff,
originally in the Sun Alliance Memorial Garden,
now demolished.

Stanway GLOUCESTERSHIRE

Can one have a favourite war memorial? For location, style, and sheer atmosphere I think Stanway would be very high on my list. The village, such as it is, is only a handful of cottages grouped in the trees around Stanway House with its neighbouring church and stunning Jacobean gatehouse, but the memorial is up on the hill at a crossroads. Here travellers climbing the Cotswold escarpment between Tewkesbury and Stow-on-the-Wold will see a yellow limestone column by Sir Philip Stott supporting a sculpture by Alexander Fisher of a romantically-realised fight between George and the dragon, where the forces of evil are being pinioned on a spear. Closer inspection reveals superb lettering cut into the warm Cotswold stone, executed by that great engraver and typographer Eric Gill.

ALFRED HE
BUGGINS·FR
BUGGINS·HE
CHARLES TH
HUBERT THO

MEN OF STANWAY
1914-1918
FOR A TOMB
THEY HAVE AN ALTAR
FOR LAMENTATION
MEMORY

FRANCE

Victoria Embankment LONDON

The Portland stone plinth by Sir Reginald Blomfield is relatively plain, the sculpture by Sir W Reid Dick extraordinary and awe-inspiring. This golden eagle balanced on a globe turns the whole monument into something almost triumphally Roman, a perfect symbol for the soaring ambitions of the RAF whose 1923 memorial this is. It accompanies Cleopatra's Needle and other monuments that stretch out from Westminster to Blackfriars on Joseph Bazalgette's Embankment.

Plymouth DEVON

This is W C Storr-Barber's memorial for the Royal Marines on The Hoe, and includes one of my favourite inscriptions, taken from Bunyan's Pilgrim's Progress:
'And so he passed over, and all the trumpets sounded for him on the other side.'

Stansted KENT

Stansted is a collection of houses and farms spread out in a cleft of the North Downs above Wrotham. There is no real village centre, but this almost naked man holding aloft a huge palm leaf is more than enough of a focal point. He was commissioned from a Budapest sculptor called Strobl and erected here in this deep country in 1923.

Lichfield STAFFORDSHIRE

The three-spires of Lichfield cathedral look down on a Garden of Remembrance, opened in 1920 on the bank of the Minster Pool, the sheet of water that gives Lichfield the impression of being a riverside cathedral town in the manner of Worcester or Hereford.

The yellow-orange ashlared Cotswold stone of the memorial is a perfect complement to the two tiers of blue slate panels that carry the names in gilt. The whole effect, with its classical pediment, Ionic pilasters and lion masks, gathers up to form a frame for the alcove with the white stone St George and the Dragon.

The designers were Bridgeman and Son of Lichfield, a name that crops up again in the story of the lone sailor up on the wall of the old library on the opposite side of the street. Bridgeman's produced eight figures to be inserted in niches on York's South Africa memorial, including this mariner who was rejected in favour of a figure holding a rope and chain instead of a rifle. It was offered to the city council who presumably were very grateful but may not have quite known what to do with it.

additional

North Weald ESSEX

This RAF aerodrome has earned its place in legend as one of the key fighter bases that took part in the Battle of Britain in 1940. The RAF left in 1958, but North Weald is still a very active airfield, as anyone driving past on the M11 will testify. The classic 1930s detached house in the background of this photograph is the Station Officer's house that stood at the original gateway. On 3rd September 1940 North Weald suffered its heaviest raid from enemy aircraft, and 60 years later to the day the first memorial to commemorate the service given by the men and women of the base (from at least seven nations) was unveiled.

There was already a memorial to the Norwegian airmen who served here, a granite obelisk unveiled by the Crown Princess of Norway, Princess Astrid, in 1952. It contains beautifully stylised figures and aeroplanes like birds and is now standing in the centre of the arc of the new memorial.

North Weald parish church contains the graves of airmen and service personnel who gave their lives in service here, and the base has the unique distinction of being the first aerodrome to suffer the fatality of an airman, three days into the war. A Hurricane pilot was shot down in the very English sounding Battle of Barking Creek.

∧ **Lowesby** LEICESTERSHIRE

This is High Leicestershire, hunting country with quiet pastures bordered by winding lanes and fox coverts. Lowesby is little more than a hall, a handful of houses and across the fields a row of red brick railway cottages next to an abandoned station. But even here the sacrifices were made, and money was found to put up the names where all would see them, a wrought iron plaque on a new set of gates for All Saints church.

> **Bassetts Pole** WARWICKSHIRE

The first post was a pole erected by Lord Bassett in 1201 to mark the boundary of Warwickshire with Staffordshire. And after the Great War this signpost arrived to do the same job at the junction of the A446 and the A453, 'erected to the memory of Captain J H W Wilkinson and his comrades of the Staffordshire Regiments…'

∧ **National Memorial Arboretum** STAFFORDSHIRE

An eagle lands in tribute to those who took part in the Berlin Air Lift that brought food and supplies to Berlin, under seige between June 1948 and May 1949.

∧ **Strand** LONDON

Here is Wren's St Clement Danes, one the best known of the churches arriving in London with the rebuilding after the Great Fire. It is now the RAF church of London and in front of each aisle window is a domed memorial shrine, each with the eagle motif and an open book in a glass case.

⌐ **Hertford**

A hart for Hertfordshire's county town, looking out from Sir Aston Webb's high plinth in Parliament Square, an open space only created in 1921, presumably to accommodate the memorial.

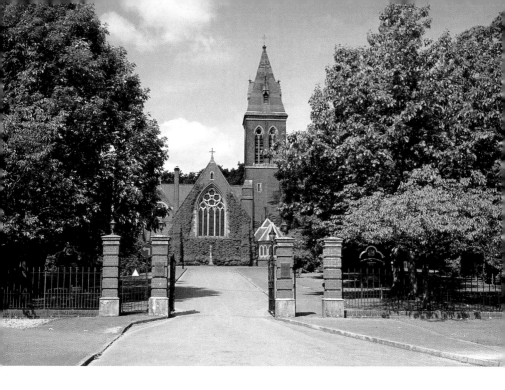

Aldershot HAMPSHIRE

Aldershot is a garrison town of barracks and parade grounds, and this is the red brick garrison church of All Saints. The avenue leading up to the church commemorates the valour of the Old Contemptibles, and the gates honour the 1st & 2nd Infantry Divisions formed in 1902. The gates were made by the apprentices and instructors at the Army Apprentices School in Arborfield, and the brick piers by students in the Royal Army Educational Corps.

< **Naseby** NORTHAMPTONSHIRE

The lion, king of beasts. Heraldic standby: rampant, sejant. Symbol of royalty, symbol of loyalty (on a football shirt at least). And here in a quiet Northamptonshire village, freeze-framed in an ironstone MGM roar. Far from the blasts and death clouds of northern France, but Naseby knows of excursions and alarums. Royal lions rose here on a June morning in 1645, only to be cut down in the most decisive battle of England's Civil War.

∟ **Woolwich** LONDON

There is no mistaking the military in Woolwich. Victorian barrack blocks, security check points, ghosts of the British soldier in every swivelling turn of a polished boot. Memorials abound, some within the confines of forbidding steel fencing, others accessible, like this Afghan and Zulu Memorial on Repository Road, a collection of rough-hewn stones raised like a cairn on the African veldt, together with an arms amnesty of stacked-up copper weapons.

> **Smithfield** LONDON

Prime beef to bully beef, cleavers to carbines: London's butchers left for war, their trade echoing behind them in the halls of Smithfield Meat Market. They are remembered still amongst all the shouts and carcass heaving that still goes on here in London's only wholesale market still in the city. Their memorial is incongruous but perfectly fitting in this atmosphere, set as it is in Lycra-coloured railings with pallets and cold store boxes leaning against it. But for how much longer? Smithfield is being stared at by calculator-eyed developers, so let's hope this memorial gives a rare pause for thought – that this is a much-loved workplace of irreplaceable character.

∧ > **Bradwell-on-Sea** ESSEX

A curious and slightly disturbing memorial out on the flatlands of the
Dengie Peninsular. Items of military hardware, or their representations,
are a very direct link to acts of almost inconceivable bravery, and this
aeroplane marks the passing of those serving at RAF Bradwell Bay.
Here Spitfires and Hurricanes were just a few of the aircraft fighting
on the front line of aerial defence in the Second World War. This
armoury also included the Mosquito, seen here painted in the colours
of RAF Northern Europe day fighter camouflage.

>> **National Memorial Arboretum** STAFFORDSHIRE

A model tank suspended in lumbering motion on the Royal Tank
Regiment memorial.

DANGER
SHARP
EDGES
Please do not climb
on the tank

9199 H41

∧ **Slapton Sands** DEVON

In 1944 a quiet corner of the South Hams coast was chosen for D-Day landing practice owing to its similiarity to the Normandy beaches. In the early hours of 28th April a convoy arrived in Lyme Bay and, as it manoeuvred into position, it was attacked by nine German torpedo boats that had evaded detection. Three American landing craft were lost, along with hundreds of men. The exact figure is still disputed, but their memorial at Torcross is this Sherman tank which had been on one of the doomed ships and was subsequently brought up from the sea bed.

National Memorial Arboretum ALREWAS, STAFFORDSHIRE
This is a kind of theme park for memorials on the banks of the River Tame. By no means a repository for war memorials, the arboretum remembers many walks of life, and just one tree can commemorate an individual. It will take many years for the trees to reach maturity, and then the monuments will be seen in their rightful sylvan context. Sections of the military are well represented, often for the first time.

⌐ An eagle for the Royal Auxilliary Air Force

∧ A polar bear for the 49th West Riding Infantry Division

∧ A silver crown for National Servicemen

∧ A blindfolded soldier stands in for those Shot at Dawn, a possibly controversial memorial to the executed who are represented behind him by wooden poles. This is not an easy place to visit: the trees are more mature and so one's thoughts can be accompanied by the sibilant sound of the wind seeking its way through the leaves.

ASTON·R·G
ATKINS·W
CARTWRIGHT·V
COOK·H·W
COOK·R

FRAZZLE·G
GREEN·A·F
HALL·H
HAYNES·E
HURREN·A·G

IRELAND·W
IRISH·F
JONES·W
KEYS·W
NASH·H·C

NEED·J
POPE·W
SMITH·W
SPALDING·W
SPARROW·L·H

WARREN·R
WILLIAMS·J
WITHERS·F

RINGERS ASSOCIATION.   IN MEMORY OF THEIR COMRADES   WHO GAVE THEIR LIVES

Worcester Cathedral

The cloisters in the cathedral were built in the 14th and 15th centuries, but the windows are Victorian with later inserts. There are countless memorials in stained glass, but here in Worcester they are particularly effective, being at eye level and surrounded by plainer glass that filters the light in from the garden outside.

Worcester Cathedral is particularly welcoming, and its cloisters are put to good use rather than just acting as a convenient walkway. What better place to remember those who played such an intrinsic part in Anglican worship. The Bell Ringers Association recalls their comrades in glass and in a metal-lettered plaque forming the sill, and nearby the Cathedral notes the lives of nine members of the Voluntary Choir and Cathedral Guild.

And so our brief tour comes almost to the end. I hope it will encourage further thought and research, and in particular a desire to see neglected and threatened memorials properly restored and protected. Even the humblest cross on a village green has extraordinary stories to tell; we must all ensure that we never forget them.

This ploughman dead in battle slept out of doors
Many a frozen night, and merrily
Answered staid drinkers, good bedmen, and all bores:
'At Mrs. Greenland's Hawthorn Bush', said he,
'I slept.' None knew which bush. Above the town,
Beyond 'The Drover', a hundred spot the down
In Wiltshire. And where now at last he sleeps
More sound in France – that, too, he secret keeps.
                    Edward Thomas: A Private

TO THE
GLORY OF GOD
AND
SACRED TO THE
MEMORY OF THE MEN
OF THE PARISH OF
ALDWINCLE
WHO FELL IN THE
GREAT WAR 1914-1918

Pte WILLIAM H.BLAND
· CHARLES BURTON
· FREDk CUNNINGTON
· FREDk HUDSON
L.CPL. A. KENNETH
MITCHELL

Pte A. PARSONS
STOKER JOHN ROLT
Pte EDWARD RICHARDSON
· REGINALD SHIELDS
Sgt J.FRANCIS SMITH
GUNr WILLIAM SPENDLOVE

Aldwincle NORTHAMPTONSHIRE

WE WILL REMEMBER THEM

Warmington NORTHAMPTONSHIRE

acknowledgements

My grateful thanks to: The British Legion, The Friends of War Memorials, Imperial War Museum, The National Memorial Arboretum, Peter Young at Lichfield City Council, Val Horsler and Rob Richardson at English Heritage, Lucy Bland, Chuck Goodwin, Nick Patterson-Gordon, Rupert Farnsworth and Biff Raven-Hill.

select bibliography

At the Going Down of the Sun, Derek Boorman, 1988
For Your Tomorrow, Derek Boorman, 1995
The War Memorials Handbook, Imperial War Museum, 2001
Buildings of England Series, Penguin, Yale University Press
The Monument Guide to England and Wales, Jo Darke, MacDonald Illustrated, 1991
Britain's Maritime Memorials & Mementoes, David Saunders, Patrick Stephens, 1996
The Architect and His Wife, A Life of Edwin Lutyens, Jane Ridley, Chatto & Windus, 2002

< Wolford Rayner was killed on the Somme on 1st July 1916. One of the 'boy' soldiers, Wolford was thought to be only 15. His name appeared on his local memorial in Barton-upon-Irwell church, Lancashire, but this has now been demolished. He will always be remembered by his family and his name is inscribed on the Thiepval Memorial in Northern France.

Port Isaac

CORNWALL

Appleby

CUMBRIA

Lower Benefield

NORTHAMPTONSHIRE

Peterborough

Leigh
KENT

Belton-in-Rutland

Gumley

LEICESTERSHIRE

Oxford

Chatteris

CAMBRIDGESHIRE